The Artist
and
Psycho-Analysis

I0480383

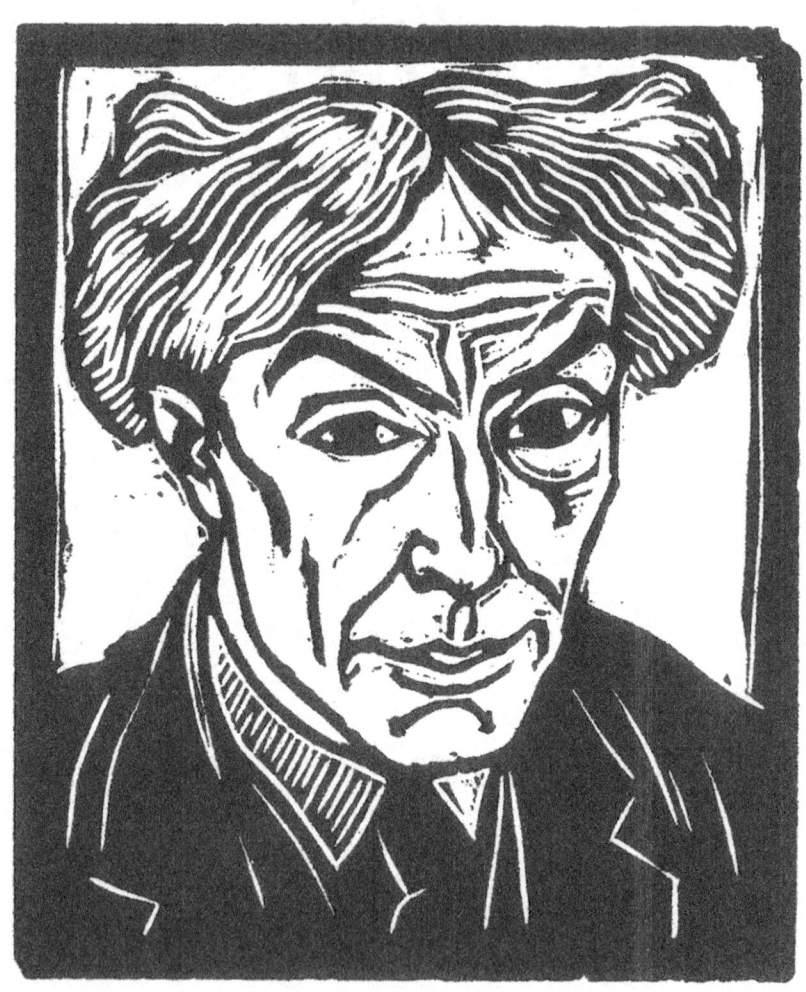

Self-portrait of Roger Fry from *Twelve Original Woodcuts by Roger Fry* published by Leonard and Virginia Woolf in 1921. David M. Rubenstein Rare Book & Manuscript Library, Duke University. Used with permission.

The Artist
and
Psycho-Analysis

ROGER FRY

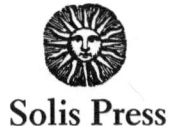

Solis Press

First published by Leonard and Virginia Woolf in 1924.
This revised edition has been completely reset with minor
spelling changes and published in 2014 by Solis Press

© Typographical arrangement is copyright of Solis Press

All rights reserved. No part of this publication may be reproduced,
stored in a retrieval system, or transmitted, in any form or by
any means, electronic, mechanical, photocopying, recording or
otherwise, except as permitted by the UK Copyright, Designs and
Patents Act 1988, without the prior permission of the publisher.

This book is sold subject to the condition that it shall not, by way or
trade or otherwise, be lent, resold, hired out or otherwise circulated
without the publisher's prior consent in any form of binding or cover
other than in which it is published and without a similar condition
including this condition being imposed on the subsequent purchaser.

ISBN: 978-1-910146-06-4

Published by Solis Press, PO Box 482,
Tunbridge Wells TN2 9QT, Kent, England

Web: www.solispress.com | *Twitter*: @SolisPress

THE ARTIST
AND PSYCHO-ANALYSIS

As I am no psychologist, my presumption in addressing a gathering of professional psychologists seems to call for apology. My defence is that of late years you have managed to make yourselves so interesting to the world at large that you have inevitably attracted the attention of outsiders. You have let off too many fireworks in your back garden to wonder that strangers have been looking over the wall.

Before the advent of Dr. Freud you worked for so long in a tranquil and almost deserted solitude that this invasion of your privacy may be a strange and disturbing experience. As an artist let me assure you that you will get accustomed to it, for we artists have always been absurdly interesting to the outside world, and are, a good many of us, by no means averse from these self-invited guests in our workshops. And to be perfectly frank psychologists are the latest disturbers of our rest and threaten to be not the least importunate.

That is one reason why I thought it might be profitable if we arranged together the terms on which you would be not only admitted, but welcomed. Those terms are very simple, they consist of one clause, namely, that before you tell us what we are doing and why we do it, we think you should take the trouble to understand what we think we are doing and why we think we do it, I know how impatient doctors are while the patient is going through his symptoms but he does generally make that concession to human nature. If after that, you can show us that we have got a mistaken notion of our own activities, that we have unconsciously rationalized them and in doing so disguised their true significance, we will listen in all humility.

What I have to suggest to you tonight is rather complicated. I will therefore begin by summarizing briefly my main ideas.

(1) The words art and artist are simple enough, but alas they have no sharply defined usage. Artists are a group of people of very different temperaments and some of them are actuated by quite different motives, and exercise quite different psychical activities, from others.

(2) I believe that two distinct aims and activities have got classed together under the word art, and that the word artist is used of two distinct groups of men. One of these groups into which I would divide artists is mainly preoccupied with creating a fantasy-world in which the fulfilment of wishes is realized. The other is concerned with the contemplation of formal relations. I believe this latter activity to be as much detached from the instinctive life as any human activity that we know; to be in that respect on a par with science. I consider this latter the distinctive aesthetic activity. I admit that to some extent these two aims may both appear in any given work of art but I believe them to be fundamentally different, if not in their origins, at least in their functions.

To begin with let us get clear about the question of origins. No doubt the question of the origin of any phenomenon is of great interest and importance, hut it must always be borne in mind that the discovery of the origin is not an explanation of the phenomenon. Origins do not necessarily explain functions. The alimentary canal and the brain both have their origin in the epithelial tissue, but one would give an enquirer a strange idea of the functional importance of the brain in the economy of the body if one only stated that it was originally part of the skin.

So if you were to prove that art originated in the sexual feelings of man, that might be a very important and interesting discovery, but it would be no explanation of the significance of art for human life. Not what an organ came from, but what it has come to be, is the most important consideration, though what it came from, and the path it has taken in its progress, may throw a light on what it really is. As an instance take the case of language. Dr. Freud in his lectures quotes a theory of language which I am not qualified to criticize or approve but which sounds to me plausible—it is that when men began to work in groups at wood-cutting, building, or what not, they sweetened their toil by shouting together sounds that had a sexual significance and that gradually these sounds become dissociated from sex and associated with particular actions or objects, and thus the original roots of language came into being. Now to argue from this that language is merely a function of the sex instinct would be grotesque. Since it has come to be the vehicle for the whole discursive intellectual life of man—it has come to serve most of all precisely those activities which are most completely removed from the instinctive life. Indeed all human activities must presumably have their ultimate origins in some part of the purely animal and instinctive life of our earliest ancestors.

Science itself, the activity of the pure reflective intellect, no doubt comes from a gradual misapplication and distortion of what was once only a weapon in the struggle for life. What was once hardly more than the animal ingenuity, which enabled man to contrive elementary devices for protection or shelter, has become through that very process of misapplication the purely reflective and disinterested intellectual power of an Einstein or a Freud, and we can show almost every intermediate stage in this long process. Now if you wanted to investigate the real nature this truth-seeking passion of scientific men, it might be important, no doubt, to discover when it first branched off from the instinctive ratiocination of animals, but you could say nothing about its significance unless you studied it beyond the point where it had lost all traces of its subservience to the instinctive life. To understand the scientific activity you must note that its essence is precisely this complete detachment from the instinctive life, its complete uselessness, its abiological nature, since it exists not to serve life but truth, and this is precisely why those who devote themselves to this activity are constantly in conflict with the mass of mankind which is deeply concerned with life and completely indifferent to truth.

Now one of the pleas I want to make to you is that, if you wish to discover something about the nature of artistic activity, you should study it at a stage where it has thrown off the traces of its origin, has run clear, as it were, of all these accessory accompaniments which surround and, perhaps, cloak it in its earlier stages.

There is such a thing as impure or useful science, and, if you were to analyse that activity, you would find all sorts of biological motives at work, although the fundamental truth-seeking passion of pure science is distinguished precisely by its independence of, and its indifference to, biological necessity.

Similarly there is an impure and, perhaps, useful art (though the use of impure art is not so easily demonstrated as that of impure science); here too, analysis would reveal a number of elements which really form no part of the essential aesthetic activity, and you will make a serious mistake if, after such an analysis, you declare these to be constituent parts of that phenomenon.

If you have a substance which you know to be chemically pure it is clear that you have a right to say that every element which you discover in that substance by analysis is a constituent part of it, but, if you have any reason to suspect an impure mixture, you know that any particular element which the analysis reveals may be due to the impurity and form no part of the substance which you are investigating.

Now that the aesthetic activity does mix in various degrees with a number of other activities is surely evident. Take for instance advertisements: many of these show no aesthetic effort and do not even try to afford aesthetic pleasure; they merely convey more or less inaccurate information about a particular object. You can think of advertisements where not only are the merits of the objects enumerated but the object, let us say a bottle of Somebody's Beer, is depicted. Every detail of the bottle and its label is given so that we may recognize it when we see it in the bar, but there is no sign that in the manner of representation any thought has been expended for our aesthetic pleasure. On the other hand I take certain advertisements in American journals, where advertisements are taken seriously and romantically, and I find a very genuine effort, in the proportion and spacing of the letters, in the harmonious consistence of the forms, and in the exact presentation of the object, towards aesthetic pleasure. None the less this aesthetic appeal is mixed with all sorts of appeals to other feelings than the love of beauty—appeals to our sense of social prestige, to our avarice, to our desire for personal display, and so forth.

Or take again the case of dress—here no doubt there is often a considerable care for pure beauty of line and harmony of colour, but such considerations have continually to give place to far more pressing concerns connected with social rivalry, in fact to all the complicated mass of instincts which go to make up what we call snobbishness.

These, then, are cases of obvious mixtures, in which the aesthetic impulse has a part—but you will say these belong to applied art; if we take pictures which subserve no ultimate use we shall surely be safe. But alas the vast majority of pictures are not really works of art at all. No doubt in most a careful analysis would reveal some trace of aesthetic preoccupations, but for the most part the appeal they make is to quite other feelings.

For the moment I must be dogmatic and declare that the aesthetic emotion is an emotion about form. In certain people, purely formal relations of certain kinds arouse peculiarly profound emotions, or rather I ought to say the recognition by them of particular kinds of formal relations arouse these emotions. Now these emotions about forms may be accompanied by other emotions which have to do more or less with what I call the instinctive life.

The simplest examples of this can be taken from music. If, as frequently happens, an unmusical child strikes six notes in succession on the piano, the chances are that no one would be able to perceive any necessary relation between these notes—they have been struck by accident, as we say. But if I strike the first six notes of "God Save The King," every one who is not quite music-deaf recognizes that they have, as one would say, a meaning, a purpose. They occur in such a sequence that after each note has been struck we feel that only certain notes can follow and, as the notes follow one another, they more or less adequately fulfil our expectation. *i.e.,* from the beginning the idea of a formal design or scheme is impressed on our minds, and anything which departed violently from that would be not merely meaningless, but an outrage to our sense of order and proportion. We have then an immediate recognition of formal design, of a trend in every part towards a single unity or complete thing which we call the tune.

Now let us suppose that you hear "God Save The King" for the first time; it is possible that you would get an emotion from the mere recognition of that formal system. I do not say it would be a very profound or important emotion, but it might be an emotion, and it would probably stir up no image whatever in your mind, would be associated with no particular person or thing or idea. But those particular notes have become associated with many other things in our minds, so that when they are played we no longer can fix our minds on the form, we are instantly invaded by the associated feelings of loyalty, devotion to country, boredom from the memory of tiresome functions, or relief that we can now at least leave the theatre. We shall say that that particular formal design of notes has become symbolical of numerous other things with which it has become associated.

Now this simple case presents in easy form some of the problems which confront us in works of art of all kinds. The form of a work of art has a meaning of its own and the contemplation of the form in and for itself gives rise in some people to a special emotion which does not depend upon the association of the form with anything else what ever. But that form may by various means either by casual opposition or by some resemblance to things or people or ideas in the outside world, become intimately associated in our minds with those other things, and if these things are objects of emotional feeling, we shall get from the contemplation of the form the echo of all the feelings belonging to the associated objects.

Now since very few people are so constituted by nature or training as to have developed the special feeling about formal design, and since everyone has in the course of their lives accumulated a vast mass of feeling about all sorts of objects, persons, and ideas, for the greater part of mankind the associated emotions of a work of art are far stronger than the purely aesthetic ones.

So far does this go that they hardly notice the form, but pass at once into the world of associated emotions which that form calls up in them. Thus, to go back to our example, the vast majority of people have no notion whether the form of "God Save The King" is finely constructed and capable of arousing aesthetic emotion or not. They have never, properly speaking, heard the form because they have always passed at once into that richly varied world of racial and social emotion which has gathered round it.

And what is true of certain pieces of music is even more true of the graphic arts. Here we have forms which quite visibly resemble certain objects in nature, and not unfrequently these objects, such for instance as a beautiful woman, are charged for us with a great deal of emotion. When to this we add that people are far less sensitive to the meaning of visible formal design than they are to audible design, we need not be surprised that pictures are almost always estimated for qualities which have nothing, or almost nothing, to do with their formal design or their aesthetic quality in the strict sense.

To satisfy this emotional pleasure in the associated ideas of images which the mass of mankind feel so strongly there has arisen a vast production of pictures, writings, music, etc., in which formal design is entirely subordinated to the excitation of the emotions associated with objects. And this is what we may call popular, commercial or impure art, and to this category belongs nowadays the vast majority of so called artistic productions. On the other hand in each generation there are likely to be a certain number of people who have a sensitiveness to purely formal relations. To such people these relations have meaning and arouse keen emotions of pleasure. And these people create such systems of formal relations and do not sacrifice willingly or consciously anything of those formal relations to the arousing of emotions connected with objects in the outside world. Their whole attention is directed towards establishing the completest relationship of all the parts within the system of the work of art.

It so happens that these systems of formal relations the meaning of which is apprehended by a comparatively few people in each generation, have a curious vitality and longevity, whereas these works in which appeal is made chiefly to the associated ideas of images rarely survive the generation for whose pleasure they were made. This may be because the emotions about objects change more rapidly than the emotions about form. But whatever the reason, the result is that the accumulated and inherited artistic treasure of mankind is made up almost entirely of those works in which formal design is the predominant consideration.

This contrast between the nature of inherited art and the mass of contemporary art has become so marked that the word "classic" is often used (loosely and incorrectly, no doubt) to denote work which has this peculiar character. People speak of classical music, for instance, when they mean the works of any of the great composers. It is significant of the rarity of comprehension of such formal design that to many people classical music is almost synonymous with "dull" music.

Now what I want to put before you is that the purposes and methods of these two kinds of art and of the two kinds of artist that produce them are so different—in so many ways so diametrically opposed that when you set out to analyse the nature and function of art by psychological tests, you must know which kind you are dealing with and you must keep your results in separate pigeon-holes or else you will only make confusion worse confounded.

Before I go any further I will turn to what one or two of the psychological authorities have said on the subject. I quote the passage in his introduction to Psycho Analysis in which Dr. Freud speaks of the artist. This is what he says:—

> "Before you leave to-day I should like to direct your attention for a moment to a side of phantasy-life of very general interest. There is, in fact a path from phantasy back again to reality, and that is—art. The artist has also an introverted disposition and has not far to go to become neurotic. He is one who is urged on by instinctive needs which are too clamorous; he longs to attain to honour, power, riches, fame, and the love of women; but he lacks the means of achieving these gratifications. So, like any other with an unsatisfied longing, he turns away from reality and transfers all his interest, and all his Libido, too, on to the creation of his wishes in life. There must be many factors in combination to prevent this becoming the whole outcome of his development; it is well known how often artists in particular suffer from partial inhibition of their capacities through neurosis. Probably their constitution is endowed with a powerful capacity for sublimation and with a certain flexibility in the repressions determining the conflict. But the way back to reality is found by the artist thus: He is not the only one who has a life of phantasy; the intermediate world of phantasy is sanctioned by general human consent, and every hungry soul looks to it for comfort and consolation. But to those who are not artists the gratification that can be drawn from the springs of phantasy is very limited; their inexorable repressions prevent the enjoyment of all but the meagre day-dreams which can become conscious.

A true artist has more at his disposal. First of all he understands how to elaborate his day-dreams, so that they lose that personal note which grates upon strange ears and becomes enjoyable to others; he knows too how to modify them sufficiently so that their origin in prohibited sources is not easily detected. Further, he possesses the mysterious ability to mould his particular material until it expresses the idea of his phantasy faithfully; and then he knows how to attach to this reflection of his phantasy-life so strong a stream of pleasure that, for a time at least, the repressions are out-balanced and dispelled by it. When he can do all this, he opens out to others the way back to the comfort and consolation of their own unconscious sources of pleasure, and so reaps their gratitude and admiration; then he has won—through his phantasy—what before he could only win in phantasy, honour, power, and the love of women."

I must ask you to believe that any criticism I make on this passage is not actuated by motives of personal pique. To be called introverted and on the brink of being neurotic does not seriously affect me. Indeed ever since I observed that the only people worth talking to, the only agreeable companions, belonged to the class that morbidly healthy, censorious people classed as neurotic and degenerate, these words have lost all terror for me. All the same I must declare that the portrait of the artist here given is drawn on the lines of a widespread popular fallacy about the "artistic temperament."

Most people lead dull, monotonous and conventional lives with inadequate satisfaction of their libido and one of their favourite phantasies is that of the Bohemian—the gay, reckless, devil-may-care fellow who is always kicking over the traces and yet gets toleration and even consideration from the world by reason of a purely magic gift called genius. Now this creature is not altogether a myth—he or something like him does undoubtedly exist—he frequently practises art but he is generally a second-rate artist. He may even be a very brilliant and successful one, but he is none the less a very minor artist. On the other hand almost all the artists who have done anything approaching first-rate work have been thoroughly bourgeois people—leading quiet, unostentatious lives, indifferent to the world's praise or blame, and far too much interested in their job to spend their time in kicking over the traces.

Now all through this passage Dr. Freud is giving us the picture of such a brilliant, successful and essentially impure artist—I need not say that I use the words pure and impure in a strictly aesthetic sense without any reference to sexual morality—*i.e.*, he is an artist who realizes the dream world wherein he and his admirers find an ideal satisfaction of their unsatisfied instincts. He creates images and situations which belong to this dream world wherein we are free to play the role which we all think we have somehow missed in actual life.

It is quite true that this explains nearly all contemporary artistic creation. You have only to think of the average novel, especially the feuilleton of papers like the *Daily Mail* and the *Daily Mirror*, and others, which supply every day their pittance of imagined romantic love to hungry girl clerks and housemaids. In fact I believe the most successful and widely read of these (mostly lady) novelists do really day-dream in print, as it were; nothing else would account for their astounding productivity. These people have the fortunate gift of dreaming the average person's day-dream so that the wish-fulfilment which comes natural to them coincides precisely with the wish-fulfilment of a vast number of the population. Other less fortunate writers have deliberately and consciously to concoct the sort of day-dream that they believe the public want, and these can never be quite the best-sellers.

None of these conditions apply to any first-rate novel—the novels that have endured do not represent wish-fulfilment to any considerable extent. They depend on the contrary for their effect upon a peculiar detachment from the instinctive life. Instead of manipulating reality so as to conform to the libido, they note the inexorable sequence in life of cause and effect, they mark the total indifference of fate to all human desires, and they endeavour to derive precisely from that inexorability of fate an altogether different kind of pleasure—the pleasure which consists in the recognition of *inevitable sequences*; a pleasure which you see corresponds to the pleasure which we found in marking the inevitable sequence of the notes in a tune; in fact again a pleasure derived from the contemplation of the relations and correspondences of form. To give you instances—no one who hoped to get an ideal wish-fulfilment would go to *Mme. Bovary* or *Anna Karenina* or even *Vanity Fair*.

Another immense art industry of today is the Cinema, and here too wish-fulfilment reigns supreme. I remember an advertisement of a Cinema with the legend "Let us live a life in two hours." This was a clear appeal to the desire to realize ideally what reality had denied, and indeed there can be no doubt about the method and purpose of nearly all the films, at least such as are not definitely comic, since the comic introduces another problem which I cannot go into now.

By a process which is mere child's play in the dream life we instantly identify ourselves with the hero, and then what satisfaction we attain! With what incredible skill and what incredible good fortune we foil the villain's plot against the heroine, arrive in the nick of time to shoot him dead, and ride off with the heroine either insensible from fear or just able to cling to us for dear life as we cross terrible ravines on a fallen tree-trunk, scale precipices and crash through forests, and always with the certainty of ultimate and triumphant success! But I needn't labour the point; the theatre with its audience always clamorous for a happy ending is a no less obvious a case.

What is more interesting is the question of the real artist's attitude to all this; for, in so far as he has to depend on his art for his living, he is under the hard compulsion of throwing a sop to the public, and therefore of giving some satisfaction to the dream-life in his creations. The whole question of the artistic conscience centres round this point. It so happens that some great artists have had rather easy artistic consciences. Dickens is a noteworthy case of this and you all know how he deliberately and consciously spoiled one of his novels by yielding to the clamour of the public and giving it a happy ending, though by doing so his broke the sequence which he knew to be aesthetically inevitable.

But the mere fact that there is such a conflict between the artist and the general public is a proof that *quâ* artist the creator has other aims than that of wish-fulfilment and that the pleasure which he feels is not thus directly connected with the libido.

Freud, however daring some of his generalizations may be, is a man of scrupulous intellectual integrity, and he has generally avoided treating the question of aesthetics and the artistic impulse, knowing, I suppose, that he has not the necessary sensibility and understanding. But other Psycho-analysts have gone further. Dr. Jung devotes a chapter of his psychological types to the artist. I wish I could criticize this, but I frankly confess I do not understand what it is about. Nothing that he says corresponds to any kind of experience which I or, I suspect, any of the artists I have ever known have ever had. In fact, I can find no connection at all with real experience so that I must simply leave it on one side, merely noting by the way that according to Jung Western art implies an extrovert attitude and Eastern art an introvert attitude (Freud you will remember makes all artists introvert). Anyone who knows Oriental and Western Art at all intimately must shudder at the temerity of any such generalization.

I quite recognize that a certain positive turn of mind makes me unfitted to follow Jung's speculations and that I am perhaps unfairly neglecting him. I turn to Dr. Pfister and here too, I will confess to a certain prejudice. I find, according to him, that psycho-analysis can only be safely practised by Christians,—all other religions are dissolved by the destructive activity of psycho-analysis—but the Christian religion has the mysterious power of remaining insoluble. This hardly reassures me that Dr. Pfister possesses that intellectual impartiality which Freud so rightly claims as the chief weapon of the man of science.

Well, Dr. Pfister has a chapter on Psycho-Analysis and Art. He had the opportunity to analyse a youth of eighteen, who had apparently come to him for treatment and who was frequently disposed to paint pictures. I will read you a description of a typical example "The Bridge of Death."

"A youth is about to leap away from a female corpse on to a bridge lost in a sea of fog, in the midst of which Death is standing. Behind him the sun rises in blood-red splendour. On the right margin two pairs of hands are trying to recall or hold back the hurrying youth!"

Would you like one more, "Night's highest hope?"

"Night sits as a mother on a rock holding her child on high. Around her lie 'spirits of the night' holding out their hands to her like praying Mahommedans. Rosy-tipped clouds announce the approaching dawn."

As a result of prolonged investigation of such works Dr. Pfister arrives at the conclusion that:—

> "Artistic or poetic inspiration is to be regarded as the manifestation of repressed desires and, as such, formed in accordance with the laws by which Freud grouped the processes participating in the origin of neurotic symptoms, dreams, hallucinations and related phenomena, save that a whole is created, the deeper psychological significance of which, however, is not perfectly clear to the artist."

"Everything was present," he adds, "poetic creation, substitution, dramatization. The most extensive use was made of symbolism."

"Everything was present," I should add, except the faintest glimmer of any artistic feeling. The one thing I should know about this interesting young man's drawings would have been the extreme improbability that he would ever be the least good as an artist.

Indeed from time to time my advice is asked about the drawings of unhappy and dissatisfied young men and women, drawings which are not altogether unlike the improvisations of this Swiss boy, and I invariably recommend them not to take up art, because I know that real artistes, even if they are destined to paint highly imaginative works and to go mad in the end like Van Gogh, generally begin by making an elaborate study of an old pair of boots or something of that kind.

I do not for a moment doubt the value of Dr. Pfister's analysis from the point of view of understanding the nervous troubles of his patient. I should think indeed, that they would be in effect as useful as the study of his dreams, but, precisely in proportion as they were valuable as indications of the patient's dream life, they were worthless as indications of the nature of real art.

For I come back to this, that nothing is more contrary to the essential aesthetic faculty than the dream. The poet Mallarmé foresaw this long before Freud had revealed the psychological value of dreams, for in his poem in memory of Theophie Gautier he says that "the spirit of Gautier, the pure poet, now watches over the garden of poetry from which he banishes the Dream, the enemy of his charge." You notice that in this connection he calls him deliberately the pure poet, knowing that in proportion as poetry becomes impure it accepts the Dream. You notice also that Dr. Pfister quite unknowingly betrays how little he knows what art is really about when he says of his patient's work that the most extensive use is made of symbolism. I have elsewhere expressed the belief that in a world of symbolists only two kinds of people are entirely opposed to symbolism, and they are the man of science and the artist, since they alone are seeking to make constructions which are completely self-consistent, self-supporting and self-contained—constructions which do not stand for something else, but appear to have ultimate value and in that sense to be real.

It is, of course, perfectly natural that people should always be look-ing for symbolism in works of art. Since most people are unable to perceive the meaning of purely formal relations, are unable to derive from them the profound satisfaction that the creator and those that understand him feel, they always look for some meaning that can be attached to the values of actual life, they always hope to translate a work of art into terms of *ideas* with which they are familiar. None the less in proportion as an artist is pure he is opposed to all symbolism.

You will have noticed that in all these psycho-analytical enquir-ies into pictorial art the attention of the investigator is fixed on the nature of the images, on what choice the painter has made of the objects he represents. Now I venture to say that no one who has a real understanding of the art of painting attaches any importance to what we call the subject of a picture—what is represented. To one who feels the language of pictorial form all depends on *how* it is presented, *nothing* on what. Rembrandt expressed his profoundest feelings just as well when he painted a carcass hanging up in a butcher's shop as when he painted the Crucifixion or his mistress. Cézanne who, most of us believe to be the greatest artist of modern times expressed some of his grandest conceptions in pictures of fruit and crockery on a common kitchen table.

I remember when this fact became clear to me, and the instance may help to show what I mean. In a loan exhibition I came upon a picture by Chardin. It was a signboard painted to hang outside a druggist's shop. It represented a number of glass retorts, a still, and various glass bottles, the furniture of a chemist's laboratory of that time. You will admit that there was not much material for wish-fulfilment (unless the still suggested remote possibilities of alcohol). Well, it gave me a very intense and vivid sensation. Just the shapes of those bottles and their mutual relations gave me the feeling of something immensely grand and impressive and the phrase that came into my mind was "This is just how I felt when I first saw Michel Angelo's frescos in the Sistine Chapel." Those represented the whole history of creation with the tremendous images of Sybils and Prophets, but aesthetically it meant something very similar to Chardin's glass bottles.

And here let me allude to a curious phenomenon which I have frequently noticed, namely that even though at the first shock of a great pictorial design the subject appears to have a great deal to do with one's emotional reaction, that part of one's feeling evaporates very quickly; one soon exhausts the feelings connected by associated ideas with the figures, and what remains, what never grows less nor evaporates, are the feelings dependent on the purely formal relations. This indeed may be the explanation of that curious fact that I alluded to, the persistence throughout the ages of works in which formal perfection is attained, and the rapid disappearance and neglect which is the fate of works that make their chief appeal through the associated ideas of the images.

At this point I must try to meet an objection which psycho-analysts are certain to raise. They will say that in my description of popular art I have used the word *wish* in the ordinary sense of a more or less conscious wish, whereas Freud uses wish of a desire which has been repressed from consciousness and remains active in the unconscious. The true Freudian wish is incapable of direct satisfaction. The typical kind of case is something like this. A middle aged lady finds herself compelled at a certain hour of the day to go into a particular room and arrange all the objects in a particular way. She cannot explain the least why she does it and why she is compelled to perform this senseless act. By psycho-analysis it is discovered that in her extreme youth she was in love with her father and wanted to kill her mother, but that this desire was repressed from consciousness and came out later on in this peculiar and roundabout way. Perhaps both father and mother were dead at the period of her illness, and so any such fulfilment would be impossible but even if alive she has ceased to love her father or be jealous of her mother.

I admit that if you adhere strictly to the use of the word "wish" in this sense, it is quite possible that Cézanne's still-life pictures are a sublimation of some such repressed instincts. But you will notice that Freud himself when he talks of the artist neglects entirely his own definition of wish. The wish in this case is the unsatisfied trying for "fame, power, money, and the love of women." Now these are not repressed wishes, they are, or may be, clearly allowed in conscious-ness, and they are capable of direct fulfilment. And he goes on to say that it is only because circumstances do not allow of their direct fulfilment that the artist takes refuge in the phantasy world. Similarly I can guess pretty clearly that Dr. Pfister's young man's inventions are inspired by unsatisfied sexual desire and this too is not repressed in the true Freudian sense. In fact I suspect that many difficulties arise from the habit of psycho-analysts of passing from the strict sense of wish to the ordinary sense without even themselves noticing how misleading the results may be. My criticisms therefore, are based on the use that they themselves make of the word in speaking of art.

Now let me assume that you have granted me my main theory at least, in its general outlines—that you admit that while there is an art which corresponds to the dream life, an art in which the phantasy-making power of the libido is at work to produce a wish-fulfilment, there is also an art which has withdrawn itself from the dream, which is concerned with reality, an art therefore which is pre-eminently *objective* and *disinterested*, and which therefore pro-ceeds in the opposite direction from the other kind of art. If you will admit this, the most interesting problems suggests themselves for solution. What is the psychological meaning of this emotion about forms, (which I will call the passion for pure beauty), and what is its relation to the desire for truth which is the only other disinterested passion we know of—what, if any, are there relations to the libido and the ego?

And here I will indicate a possibility which will have to be considered, a possibility which has often occurred to me, but with regard to which I have never come to any conclusion. I have admitted from the first the great probability, to me almost a certainty, that all psychic energy is divided ultimately from the instinctive life and has its source in the satisfaction, at however distant a remove, of some instinctive need or desire. I suppose, but I do not know, that you would trace the love of abstract truth to the reality principle, although, in its higher forms, it has long lost any biological value and has become an end in itself.

I should not be surprised if you were ultimately to trace the love of abstract beauty to the libido, but, even if you should, I should expect you to notice that its relation to that instinctive need is very different from the simple relation of the phantasy-making, dream-like quality of impure, image-making art. For whereas dream-art, if I may use the phrase, is nearly akin to the day-dream and may almost be reckoned as part of the actual instinctive life, the love of beauty implies an almost complete detachment from personality and from the wishes made by our unsatisfied libido.

Even if it derives from the libido, it does not seek to satisfy it directly in any way. None the less the question occurs what is the source of the affective quality of certain systems of formal design for those who are sensitive to pure form. Why are we moved deeply by certain sequences of notes which arouse no suggestion of any experience in actual life? Why are we moved deeply by certain dispositions of space in architecture which refer so far as we can tell to no other experience?

One thing I think we may clearly say, namely, that there is a pleasure in the recognition of order, of inevitability in relations, and that the more complex the relations of which we are able to recognize the inevitable interdependence and correspondence, the greater is the pleasure; this of course will come very near to the pleasure derived from the contemplation of intellectual constructions united by logical inevitability. What the source of that satisfaction is would clearly be a problem for psychology.

But in art there is, I think, an affective quality which lies outside that. It is not a mere recognition of order and inter-relation; every part, as well as the whole, becomes suffused with an emotional tone, Now, from our definition of this pure beauty, the emotional tone is not due to any recognizable reminiscence or suggestion of the emotional experiences of life; but I sometimes wonder if it nevertheless does not get its force from arousing some very deep, very vague, and immensely generalized reminiscences. It looks as though art had got access to the substratum of all the emotional colours of life, to something which underlies all the particular and specialized emotions of actual life. It seems to derive an emotional energy from the very conditions of our existence by its revelation of an emotional significance in time and space. Or it may be that art really calls up, as it were, the residual traces left on the spirit by the different emotions of life, without however recalling the actual experiences, so that we get an echo of the emotion without the limitation and particular direction which it had in experience.

But these are the wild speculations of an amateur. It is just here that we are waiting and longing for you to step in with your precise technique and your methodical control.

I do not pretend that either artists or art critics have made much of a job of aesthetics. We have started innumerable theories and abandoned them again without getting at any very positive and assured results. But we have of late, I think, been able to make a little clearing in the approaches to these problems by analysing a little more clearly than the older writers what goes on inside us when we are confronted by different kinds of works of art and by knowing, or trying to know, or thinking we know, what, as artists, we are after.

I expect and desire that you will test everything which we say about ourselves and our aims as ruthlessly as you test your patients' statements about their own motives, but at least I hope I have shown that it is important to know what class of objects we have in view when we talk of works of art; to know that, if you analyse the pictures of let us say the Royal Academy, your remarks may interest us on other grounds, but not for the light they throw on the aesthetic process in itself.

A CONTEMPORARY REVIEW

The following is a contemporary review published in *The Criterion: A Quarterly Review*, Volume III, Number XI, pages 471–2, April 1925. This was a literary journal edited by T. S. Eliot that was produced from 1922 to 1939. The first issue included Eliot's poem *The Waste Land* and it received contributions from many well-known writers. Eliot said of the magazine that "for pure snootiness it beats anything I have ever seen" and later said it was "possibly the best literary paper we have ever had".

The Artist and Psycho-Analysis. **By Roger Fry. (Hogarth Press.) 2s. 6d.**

MR. ROGER FRY has a theory of art which we believe to be wrong, but like many wrong theories it is held with great sincerity and is therefore expressed with great clarity. He believes in the existence of a specific aesthetic emotion; he believes that this emotion is an emotion about form; and that it is this formal element which alone gives vitality to art. He goes so far as to say that "to one who feels the language of pictorial form all depends on *how* it is presented, *nothing* on what." And finally he betrays himself by saying that a picture by Chardin, representing a number of glass retorts, a still, and various glass bottles, gave him "the feeling of something immensely grand and impressive"; and the phrase that came into his mind was: "This is just how I felt when I first saw Michelangelo's frescoes in the Sistine Chapel." This is not the occasion to examine Mr. Fry's theory of art extensively; we will merely suggest that it is the obverse of sentimentality; that it reduces the criteria of art to merely instinctive physical reactions; that, in fact, it only accounts for one element of art, whereas art is dual, consisting not solely of systems of formal relations (which are, however, essential), but also of mental attitudes. Mr. Fry's theory lacks a scale of values. For that reason he cannot distinguish between Chardin's bottles and the Sistine frescoes. But there is a wide and incalculable difference, and it is the difference between a mind and a mere sensibility.

But Mr. Fry is right to purge art of its "associated ideas of images." To anyone who sees the immense importance and utility of Freud's general theory, nothing is so dismaying as the utter futility of *all* the psycho-analysts in the presence of art. They cannot understand that art is a triumph over neurosis, and that the symbolistic and mystical imaginings which they ask us to consider as art are the very denial of art, lacking order, form, and discipline. Mr. Fry has made this distinction very clear, insisting "that nothing is more contrary to the essential aesthetic faculty than the dream. ... In a world of symbolists only two kinds of people are opposed to symbolism, and they are the man of science and the artist, since they alone are seeking to make constructions which are completely self-consistent, self-supporting, and self-contained—constructions which do not stand for something else, but appear to have ultimate value and in that sense to be real."

Mr. Fry concludes with a speculation which he puts forward very diffidently, but which is deserving of serious consideration. He wonders if the response (he calls it "the emotional tone") which we derive from formal beauty may not get its force "from arousing some very deep, very vague, and immensely generalized reminiscences." Kept to the plane of experience, this is a very plausible theory; but Mr. Fry will drag in emotion—"emotional colours of life," "emotional significance in time and space," echoes and residual traces of emotions in life. We feel that once more the sentimentalist is betraying himself, but not, however, before making a few distinctions and definitions of very great value.

HERBERT READ.

www.ingramcontent.com/pod-product-compliance
Lightning Source LLC
Chambersburg PA
CBHW072034230526
45468CB00021B/1810